Rainforests

Lucy Beckett-Bowman

Designed by Samantha Meredith

Illustrated by Natalie Hinrichson

Reading consultant: Alison Kelly, Roehampton University

Rainforest consultant: Dr. Julia Jones, Bangor University

Contents

In the rainforest

Tropical rainforests are thick, leafy jungles. They grow in warm places where it rains a lot.

Many different plants, animals and people live in them.

Towering trees

Plants and trees need sunlight to grow.

The branches of the tallest trees are spread out so that their leaves get plenty of sunlight. This layer is called the canopy.

Some of the biggest trees in rainforests are over 1,000 years old.

Less sunlight reaches this layer. It is called the understorey. The plants here have big leaves to catch as much light as they can.

The forest floor is dark, so there aren't many plants.

Canopy climbers

The canopy layer is full of life. Some of the animals that live there never go down to the forest floor.

Sloths have long, sharp claws that help them hang from branches. They move very slowly and spend most of their lives asleep.

Howler monkeys gather in groups at the tops of the trees.

They hang from their tails, and pick fruit and leaves to eat.

They howl loudly to warn other monkeys to keep away.

Aye-ayes have long middle fingers that they use to pull bugs out of branches.

In the understorey

Beneath the canopy, the trees are covered with different kinds of plants.

Hummingbirds use their long beaks to feed from orchids.

The roots of these plants soak up water from the air.

Some plants fill up with water. Frogs sometimes lay their eggs in them.

Woody vines, called lianas, grow up trees to get closer to the sunlight.

These leaves have pointed 'drip tips', so that water runs off them quickly.

On the ground

Millions of bugs live beneath the trees, on plants and on the forest floor.

Leafcutter ants bite leaves into small pieces.

The ants carry the pieces to their nest, then chew them into a pulp.

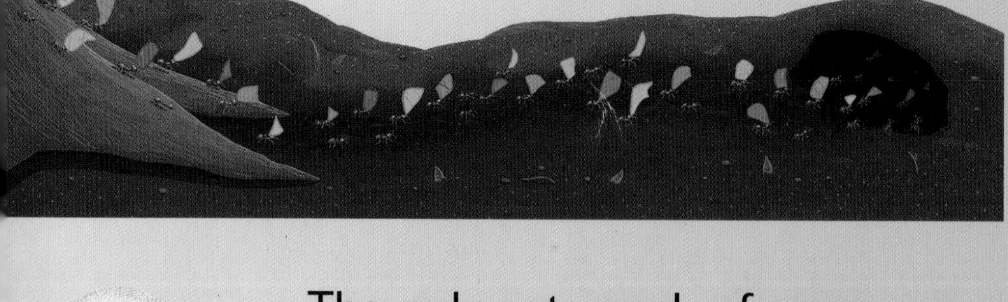

The pulp rots, and a fungus grows on it. The ants eat the fungus.

Gladiator spiders weave sticky nets to drop onto their prey.

This Brazilian wandering spider has caught a bug and bitten it with its poisonous fangs.

Getting about

Many animals travel through the rainforest without touching the ground.

Flying frogs have long legs and wide, webbed feet.

They jump from a branch, then glide through the air to another tree.

Gliding snakes can leap from tree to tree. They steer in the air by wiggling their bodies.

A baby spider monkey clings to its mother's tummy. The mother uses her arms and tail to swing through the trees.

A flying squirrel sits on a tree branch.

It leaps into the air...

...then stretches out its arms and legs, and glides to another branch.

Big beasts

Some large rainforest animals hunt other animals for food.

This jaguar is prowling around on the forest floor, looking for prey such as deer and pigs.

An anaconda quietly slithers up to a tapir by a river.

It wraps itself around the tapir and squeezes tightly.

Gorillas are huge, powerful animals, but they just like to eat plants.

The anaconda opens its jaws and slowly swallows the tapir.

After its huge meal, the snake doesn't eat for several months.

After dark

Some animals sleep during the day and only come out at night.

A red-eyed tree frog wakes up to feed. It catches insects with its long tongue.

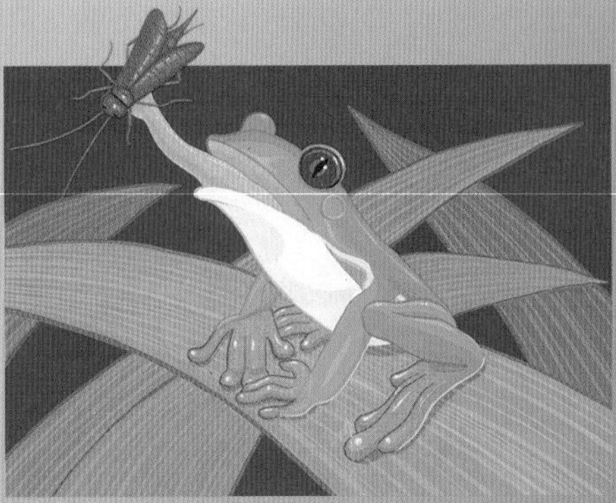

An owl hears the frog moving and swoops down from a tree to catch it.

The frog shows its bright body and eyes to surprise the owl, then escapes.

Tarsiers have huge eyes so they can see when there isn't much light.

They catch insects with their long fingers, then eat them.

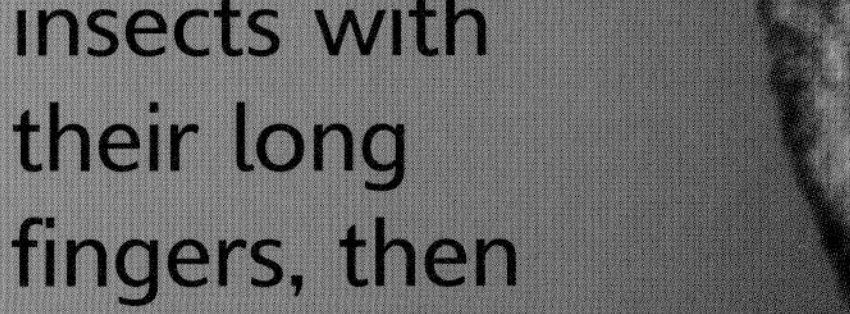

With so many creatures, rainforests can be very noisy at night.

Smelly plants

Rainforest plants can attract insects with their smell.

Rafflesia flowers can be as big as truck wheels. They smell like rotting meat to attract flies. The flies spread the flower's pollen.

A fly is attracted to a pitcher plant by its strong smell.

The fly lands on the waxy edge of the leaf. It slips inside into a special liquid.

The fly's body dissolves until it is liquid too. It is now food for the plant.

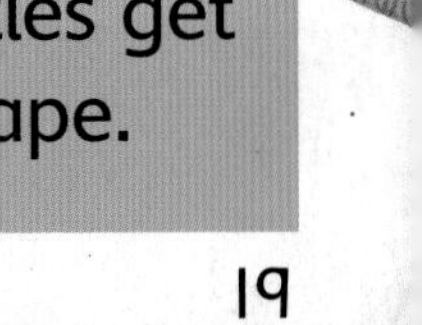

Some water lilies trap beetles when they close their petals at night. The beetles get covered in pollen and then escape.

Beaky birds

Rainforest birds have beaks in many shapes and sizes. They are good for different things.

This macaw has a strong beak that can pierce fruit and crack nut shells.

Harpy eagles are so big they can grab monkeys out of trees. They eat them with their sharp, hooked beaks.

Toucans have long beaks. They can pick berries that are hard for other birds to reach.

Rainforest rivers

Many rainforests have large rivers running through them. The most famous is the Amazon, in South America.

Lots of animals live and hunt in the Amazon.

Capybaras have large front teeth for nibbling long grass.

Scarlet ibises use their long beaks to find food in the mud.

Caimans hunt with only their eyes and noses above water.

Piranhas have sharp teeth that they use to tear animal flesh.

Rich rainforests

Rainforest plants can provide food and other useful things.

The seeds in cocoa pods are used to make a paste called cocoa butter.

Cocoa butter is used to make candles...

soap...

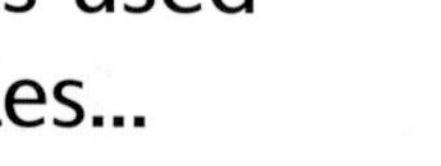

and chocolate.

Bananas were first found in rainforests.

This bud will unfold, and the flowers inside will turn into bananas.

Some people chew the leaves of the Kawakawa plant to cure toothache.

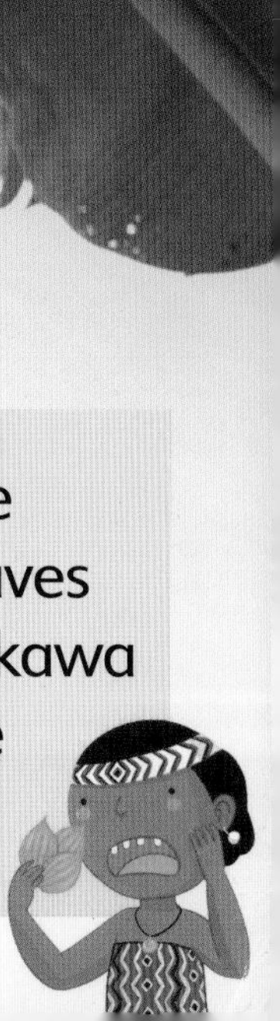

Tropical tribes

Groups of people, called tribes, have lived in rainforests for thousands of years.

The people in this photo built their home with wood and reeds from the rainforest.

They live near a river, so the house is on stilts in case the river floods.

People search in rainforests for fruit that they can eat, such as mangoes.

Men hunt animals to eat, using spears, bows and arrows, and blow pipes.

Boats carry people and goods quickly through the rainforest.

Ruining rainforests

Rainforests could be lost forever because so many trees are being cut down.

People use the wood to make things such as paper and furniture.

The land is also cleared so that farmers can grow crops and keep cows.

When rainforests are destroyed, animals like these orang-utans lose their homes.

If an animal dies out forever, it becomes extinct.

Bali tigers lost their rainforest home, and are now extinct.

Glossary of rainforest words

Here are some of the words in this book you might not know. This page tells you what they mean.

tropical - hot, rainy weather. Rainforests grow in tropical places.

canopy - a thick layer of leaves and branches at the top of tall trees.

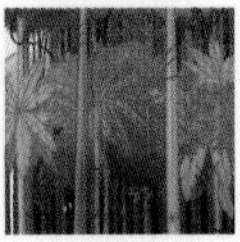
understorey - the part of a rainforest between the canopy and the ground.

liana - a woody vine that grows up a tree towards the sunlight.

drip tips - pointed tips on leaves that help water to run off them.

pollen - a powder that plants use to make seeds.

extinct - when animals and plants die out and there are no more left.

Websites to visit

You can visit exciting websites to find out more about rainforests.

To visit these websites, go to the Usborne Quicklinks Website at **www.usborne-quicklinks.com** Read the internet safety guidelines, and then type the keywords "**beginners rainforests**".

The websites are regularly reviewed and the links in Usborne Quicklinks are updated. However, Usborne Publishing is not responsible, and does not accept liability, for the content or availability of any website other than its own. We recommend that children are supervised while on the internet.

Chameleons change their skin to different shades to show what kind of mood they are in.

Index

Acknowledgements

Photographic manipulation by John Russell

Photo credits

The publishers are grateful to the following for permission to reproduce material:
© **Ingo Arndt/Minden Pictures/FLPA** 18; © **Cn Boon/Alamy** 25; © **Jean Paul Ferrero/ardea.com** 29; © **Michael Fogden/Oxford Scientific** 12; © **David Haring/DUPC/Photolibrary** 17; © **Steve Kaufman/Corbis** 20; © **Frans Lanting/Corbis** Cover; © **Buddy Mays/Corbis** 6-7; © **Gavin Parsons/ardea.com** 2-3; © **Ken Preston-Mafham/Premaphotos** 10-11; © **Anup Shah/naturepl.com** Cover; © **Shattil & Rozinski/Naturepl** 14-15; © **Kevin Schafer/Alamy** 31; © **Paul A. Souders/Corbis** 1; © **Steve Vidler/Photolibrary** 22; © **Staffan Widstrand/naturepl** 21; © **Alison Wright/Robert Harding** 27.

First published in 2008 by Usborne Publishing Ltd., Usborne House, 83-85 Saffron Hill, London EC1N 8RT, England. www.usborne.com
First published in America 2008. U.E. Printed in China.

Sun, Moon and Stars

Farm animals

Elizabeth I

RUBBISH AND RECYCLING

Dogs

Horses and ponies

Spiders

Planes
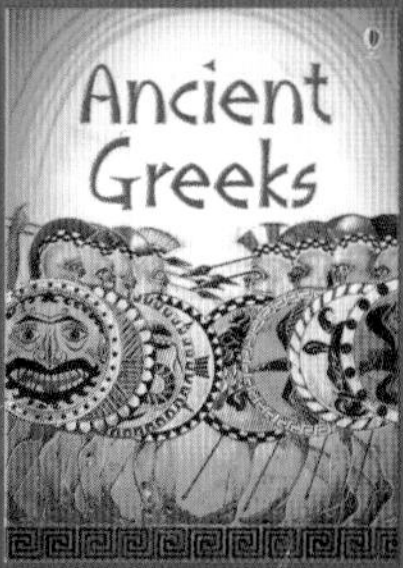
Ancient Greeks

Cats

VOLCANOES

DINOSAURS
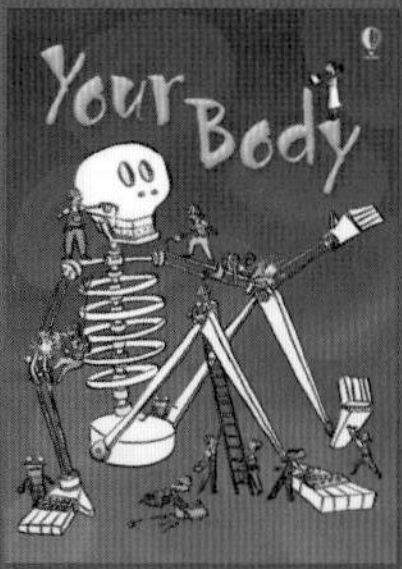
Your Body

Armour

Sharks

Celts

Vikings

Castles

How flowers grow

Knights

Living in space

Caterpillars and Butterflies

Ballet

Pirates
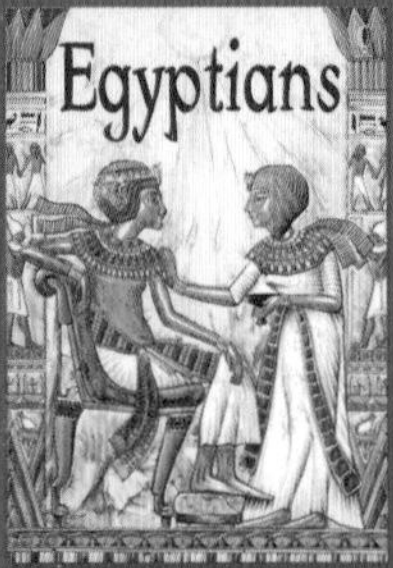
Egyptians

Eggs and Chicks
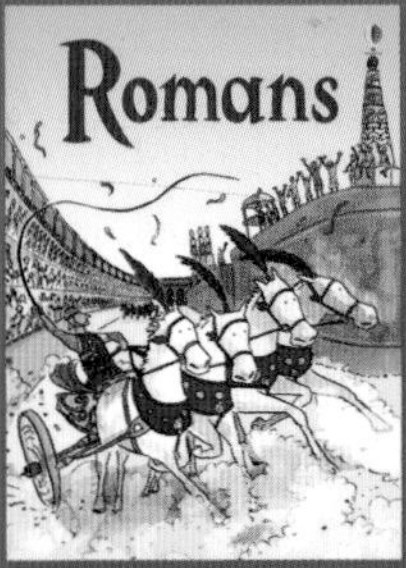
Romans

Weather

Tadpoles and frogs

Why do we eat?

Under the sea

Bears